Curiously in Love with Him

Curiously in Love with Him

To Believe Is to Receive

SHIRLEY SCHWIER

RESOURCE *Publications* • Eugene, Oregon

CURIOUSLY IN LOVE WITH HIM
To Believe Is to Receive

Resource Publications
An Imprint of Wipf and Stock Publishers
199 W. 8th Ave., Suite 3
Eugene, OR 97401

www.wipfandstock.com

PAPERBACK ISBN: 979-8-3852-7643-1
HARDCOVER ISBN: 979-8-3852-7644-8
EBOOK ISBN: 979-8-3852-7645-5

VERSION NUMBER 03/30/26

CONTENTS

THIS IS A DAYDREAM ABOUT HIM

An introduction.
A subtle description.
A gently braised canvas.
A 50-page photo-album.
A text message between myself and best friend.
A three-minute dance.
A brief hello and quick goodbye.
A gaze versus a stare.
A slight touch of the keys.
A soft kiss on the cheek.
A whisper, even.
A microscopic lens looking in.
The simplicity and knottiness of a children's book.
The fading afternoon tea.
The fleeting "it was meant to be."
The looking once more but it was too late.
The realization that no one was there to spare.
Why does it take for everyone to leave to realize He is the
only one who never really leaves.

SO, HOW TALL IS HE?

What do you mean? He's as tall as He can be.

In fact, He's so tall that is all I can see.

No matter how high I may reach as I jump, jump, and jump, He is all I can see.

And that is fine with me because now I can kick up my feet.

I didn't enter this world to guide myself, nor can I.

I didn't enter this world to figure it out, it already is.

When I arrived, I was given a map.

I lost it once but now that I have been given another, I keep it close.

Getting lost isn't hard.

I now follow the map and walk my walk.

Which way are you taking?

HE'S QUITE THE QUIET

Some say He speaks often.

Some say He does not speak at all.

I guess it is time for me to say; and I say, He speaks as He likes.

If you are hardly listening, how will you perceive?

If you are always speaking, will you be able to hear?

All things that become entangled become unentangled or simply perish.

Like my hands tied to my feet or a caged bird awaiting the feast.

I believe that means we have a choice to make, and both options can seem equally hard.

No one wants to do what is diverted but doesn't someone, eventually?

If ears are to the mind what the mouth is to the stomach, then we should be ahead of the game.

I'd say.

HE'S DIFFERENT

He doesn't break His promises.

He does not break them, and He does not forget them, even if we do.

He reminds me of His promises once my visibility of Him begins to fog.

He cares about the good I seem to have forgotten.

He is never out to get me.

He's my safe place. My best bet.

No need for a jackpot, His streets are made of gold.

My money maker, the one who has made of me a dream chaser.

Regarding Him, I don't mention a guarantee because there's nothing else, He can be but sure!

My protector, He's always taking good care of me.

I have no ask because needs continue in their absence.

Lack never presents itself because He is always there.

HOW BEAUTIFUL IS HE?

Breathtaking, you mean.

He's my sweetest treat.

Beautiful, indeed, is He.

Mm, Breathtaking, I mean.

It is not a beauty you can display on a frame or paint and try to show others.

There's no picture, no video or recording.

There is no interchangeable evidence but His voice.

You'll have to experience this one for yourself.

To perceive and to dream. Mesmerizing is He.

The "One" wants to converse with me? I'll pick Him.

Any place, at any time.

THE PRETTIEST FLOWER OF THE FIELD

That's what He calls me. I've never felt this special.

Though the field is full of blooms, He reassures me.

He recites my worth.

Reminding me of His continuous love.

He doesn't leave me to guess; it is always clear.

He doesn't allow me to doubt His devotion to me.

He often asks me to hang out.

I get dressed, put on my prettiest dress, and I know the rest will be the best story yet.

MESSAGES AT MY DOOR

Arise! Arise!

Let's conquer the day, He says.

And what should I reply?

With a simple and warm "Okay."

I agree with all that He ever says.

His words are always good and promising.

It all adds up; so, I simply trust.

His voice
His character
His choice

He has chosen me.

To love me, to lead and guide me.

He chose to die for me.

The mystery, the secrets.

He will share them at the right time.

Like a ripening grape turning into sweet wine.

WHAT DOES HE LOOK LIKE?

A. It's a mystery.

Q. Well, how old is He? A. Are you listening to me?

Q. Then, What's His name? A. Many things.

Q. Where is He from? A. Between near and far.

Q. Is He coming back? A. Yes.

Q. When? A. There is no telling.

Q. Does He know how to cook? A. He cooks all the time.

BUT WHY HIM?

Have you ever been the only person in the world?

Running, suffering, reaching but there was nothing ahead.

Have you ever been in a state beyond frost?

Frozen both in mind and in time.

Been stuck in an endless replay?

Expecting change but noticing it does not come from within?

Not your hands, not your arms, not by your own strength.

It does not exist.

What is true, what is pleasing and acceptable is not from this place.

Therefore, it certainly cannot be found from within.

Put to practice that which came from above.

That's why it is Him. That is why He came.

To reach from above that which is from within.

HE AWAITS LATE FOR ME

Don't misunderstand.

You see, He is never really late.

If He ever awaits late, it is simply because of me.

How could I ever leave my best gift at a standstill.

I say, "Thank you, my Lord," because you have never left or forsaken me.

In my sandpit I sat.

You removed up to the very last grain of sand off my skin.

Today, I choose to not keep Him waiting.

Though, He'll never change His ways.

"Don't leave me," says the world behind.

I became your orphan the day that I arrived.

CLOSE YOUR EYES

As I listen for the rain, He speaks.

My eyes begin to gaze into the light that cannot be played again by technology.

A reflection.

His voice roams through the dark skies and I try to find Him but there isn't a reply.

I fear neither the unseen nor lightning.

He inspires me as the rain lands gently and at the same time harshly.

He is the aide to my itch. He quenches my thirst.

He eliminates any lie of the things He has not said or told.

Though it is cold, I fail not to be warm.

There is no place I'd rather be than gone in this very moment towards the big and the deep blue sea.

Just as I sink in the pool or the open waters of the Sea, I can't hear a thing, and it is just Him and me.

WHAT ELSE?

Once you reach the end, that is it.

However long that moment lasts, once time is up, that is all you will get.

It will never return so just make sure you live life the right way.

Whenever you believe you have enough time the ending begins to creep in.

This is for you to realize that being intentional should be within the "everyday" everything.

This was not your chance at life to make it about you, but instead, others.

Being intentional. Being purposeful.

That's rewarding.

First, in your heart.
Second, the next life to come.

I FANTASIZE OVER HIS LOOK

I wonder as He looks at me. What do you see?

Someone sweet yet savory, full of character, a warm spice and refreshing as can be. Mi Canela.

It is impossible for Him to make mistakes.

Have you stepped back and acknowledged life today?

Seriously.

Don't say a word and don't make a sound.

Use your eyes and use your ears.

Take it all in, tell me, what do you see, and what do you hear?

Isn't it beautiful!

Breathe, breathe, breathe. Inhale it all in.

Life!

Life, indeed.

HOW MY DAY BEGINS

Most days, as I wake up, I look straight towards the sun.

I want to be embraced in warmth.

Fresh in mind, and nothing to put my cares upon.

Extending my arms slowly, I join the swaying of the trees as the breeze teaches me.

As the birds chirp along and sing their favorite song, my ears tingle and begin to move.

I stare at the bright and blue sky and wait for His first "Hi."

A glass of freshly squeezed oranges He brings to me.

His garden full of fruits, flowers and the best scenery.

What an abundant place to be.

I remain dreaming in quiet and peace.

His stillness does not allow for anything else to intervene.

This is how perfectly my day begins.

HE REMINDS ME THAT I AM PRETTY

As the sun sits far upon the never-ending ocean, so is He.

Near, and yet out of reach.

Whenever I dream too small, He dreams big for me.

He is truly all I need.

Now, how can two be?

The gentlest and the most powerful.

No one can resist His glory.

It's wanting the greatest and most far-fetched dream to conceive.

To be kissed by a wave.

I couldn't get to Him, so He traveled despite me.

To be found by the only One who could have ever made a way.

He sees my wild ideas and doesn't question me.

Simply, He redirects me.

He acknowledges my dreams and makes a way for me to
experience the best journey there could ever be.

THE CROWD

Wait!

Don't go. It's a stampede.

There's only one way it'll go.

You amongst all, becomes you small and fragile within this huge and loud crowd.

Most people don't agree with me but if you incline just a little bit.

I'd rather yell, scream and exhaust all that is within me just for you to not lose track of this voice.

He, whom it is written about, but I cannot show.

So, please, just listen.

AS HE SPEAKS, I FALL ASLEEP

And so, I begin to dream.

There is a star, and it shines ever bright.

No, it is not yellow, and it is not white.

There are not enough colors to describe.

A gaze latches onto me which I cannot break.

As I become invited into its nature, in disbelief of that which I did not know was a reality.

I lay on the comfiest clouds, and He tells me to wait.

His hand, as soft as could be. He caresses my cheek.

A mountain holding all of me.

I roll down the hills.

The pastures are full of their silk.

It's my favorite place to be.

Come, witness this with me.

Let's roll around in this heavenly dream.

I cannot wait to go to sleep!

THE SAFETY SIGN ON THE STREET

I don't need a map.

I have recently learned that the passenger seat is where I've always wanted to be.

It's the dream compared to the nightmare of the driver's seat.

To simply stare out the window.

Counting the clouds and the cows.

Following the ups and downs of the hills.

Trying to catch the sun but it never prevails.

No, I don't need a map or the steering wheel.

Give it to Him for whom it was made.

Everyone's license revoked and His has no expiration date.

CURIOUS, CURIOUS, CURIOUS

Curious, is me.

As I think what He has created for us to be.

He says He can count the number of hairs upon my head but as I detangle, that number would begin to change.

I would think …

I like to hear stories about "The Beginning."

It's the one no one knows much about but only to picture it as we dream.

He created me. Isn't that intriguing!

But not just me. Also, my mom, my pet, the flowers I picked up today and the dolphins at sea.

Quite interesting yet unable to receive.

To receive understanding, I mean.

The intricate details that, because of the Sun, we are all able to see.

As it leaves, who will be able to guide me?

HE TAUGHT ME LOVE

His words, so sweet.

His touch, the most redeeming.

His gentleness, so soothing.

His care, the most encouraging.

His kindness, beyond generous.

His grace, the most important.

His pruning, the most life changing.

His perfect plan, the most rewarding.

His investment in me, the most memorable.

His provision, so abundant.

His direction, the most specific.

His creativity, so effortless.

His ability to know me.

His most precious gift, walking right beside me.

OVERCOMPLICATED

To overcomplicate is to untie your shoe to run.

To overcomplicate is to be hungry and not accept food.

To overcomplicate is to have a peanut allergy and eat a PB&J anyway.

To overcomplicate is to know an answer exists but choose to ignore it.

To the Overcomplicates, my natural desire to know asks why.

But the disappointment strikes my gut before I even try to let the words out.

"Sorry" does not make what happened go away.

"Ignoring" does not take back the mess you made.

"Not Caring" teaches you that you will one day.

"I did not know," even if you truly did not know, will still pay out what was bought with your actions and words.

Now, here's the double swinger:

One: You can't reverse it or take it back. Please be mindful of your everyday mishaps.

Two: Though you cannot reverse it or take it back, there is One that can.

SACRIFICE

Hey, don't run away from me.

I know you have already heard, and it is not how it seems.

Once you are served with its merit you may want to flee.

One thing is certain, the payout in return is for eternity.

You can be unsure, uncertain and believe there is not enough might within you.

That's trespassing.

When we become concerned with the things that are certain to defeat and measure our strength upon it instead of His.

Whose hands no one can reach.

His speed?

There's no tool or device we can create that would compete.

So, what will you choose, Victory or Defeat?

Both exist but only one is crowned upon Him.

AND IF I HAVE NOTHING AT ALL

Not a thing to give and not a thing to say. Please, don't take anything else from me.

Not a look, not a wave. Not a smile to share reciprocate.

The missing vital sign.

I'm trying to gasp for air.

But there it is, keep moving steady with me, and not a different beat.

The sign of life that was thought to be long gone. Fold me in.

Enclose me in your tightest grip.

This is a must and no other can be.

The inevitable.

I had nothing else and yet He gave to me.

Where choice is all I had but even that was reproved.

Who ever said the rejected are too far to lose?

No, not for Him. There is never a "too late" for Him.

I CAN'T

"Can't" what?

I've never heard of such a thing.

What does "Can't" mean?

It means having flour and no other to accompany.

Having teeth and not biting.

Having eyes and not seeing.

Having hands and not eating.

And yet, bread was delivered. Because it was never up to me.

IF YOU ARE NOT HIM, I AM WILLING TO WAIT

She sits by the window as the drizzle begins its stream.

A touch of the shoulder, "Pardon Mademoiselle, is there someone you are waiting for?"

She turns to see whom that could be.

Looking into His eyes in disbelief that her dream is now within reach.

Now, where have you been? I've waited for you, my Prince, day after day.

He replies, "Oh, darling of mine. It was not yet time to make my grand entrance, that is, in your heart."

But don't look back and do look ahead.

What is greater, better and what once was worth the wait has now come.

Prepare yourself, there's a journey you are about to take.

Let's leave this tower and make way to Le Palais Royal.

WHAT ELSE WOULD YOU LIKE FROM ME?

Answers.

Don't all? But you are not like them all. I am not the provider of those.

Clarity.

I'd never lead you astray.

Understanding!

All you need is right here. No need to dig deeper for the deep.

Truth!

That's who He is. Let me introduce to you..

Why is this so difficult?!

Oh, but He has traded your "hard" for His "easy."

He's given you His whole heart.

In the midst of Him giving, all we must do is receive.

Now, how about you hold this for me until I return.

And remember to not let go.

NOW, WHERE WERE WE?

We have been right here, talking about nothing else but Him.

Taking on the journey to discover the undiscoverable is quite the adventure of life.

You will not find many there.

There is no one to tell you whether you are right or if you are wrong.

For just as they, you do not know where you are headed or what is in front.

Don't look for the end.

You will never reach it, but it will always reach you.

The "when" is never in our court.

That is why what you set in your mind is the most important of all.

Perspective.

How is it that you are viewing the world and everyone in it?

I do not seek for the things which I can see.

Everything I have is all I need.

Enjoy your daily portion, I must repeat.

The end isn't near, and neither is it far.

Count what you do have and not what you lack.

ARREST ME

Take them.

Take my hands, tie them up and arrest me.

This has been the only time in which being guilty has fit me.

Take my hands, wrap them up and throw me into that dungeon where others like I await.

If this, which you have accused me of is to never be proclaimed, then yes, here I am.

Arrest me. Here are my hands.

This I will not run from. This I am sure of.

Life without Him is prison itself. Your dark cave is not a match for me.

If I am put behind bars that restrain me, well, let me remind you again that those metal bars are nothing but fragile to Him.

Instead of breaking them down He simply commands them to open.

And indeed, they shall open.

THE IMPOSTER

And you are?

Who invited you and who let you in?

I don't remember your name on the list nor am I familiar with your face.

Please, let me help you to the door. You cannot stay.

I know my Father's voice and yours is not His.

There are similarities but a fool is simply just a fool presenting to be like Him.

My Father says to be kind to all, so here.

Take this with you on your way out.

Though you found yourself a way in, I'll kindly forgive you and hope this won't happen again.

I AM CONTENT

I don't seek any further.

I don't search for more.

I am satisfied right here.

If complete I am, there would not be enough room to accept the new.

Therefore, I don't accept.

I don't go to sleep hungry but always filled.

I don't spend my days wanting but counting just how much.

This specific journey I wasn't born in yet led.

There was a time I thirst.

There was a time I craved.

There was a time where enough was never enough.

He showed me that everything else that is out there is as good as a half-filled, airy bag of chips.

I now invest my change a bit differently these days.

WHAT DID HE SAY TODAY?

I told you everything that I could.

It's as if we sang our ABCs.

It's the same song on repeat.

The endless loop that continues to reach.

Don't turn it down, instead turn the volume up.

The lyrics never change so you aren't bound to forget.

What are numbers to letters?

They are completely different and yet used in the same context.

In Math, Science, and Texts.

But maybe, as letters interact in the same space as numbers and without each other, readings may read wrong.

Just maybe, I can be the number, and you be the letter.

Though we have our differences, we can hold hands and allow for a few things to make sense.

LIFE

Fill me up, life!

Fill me up!

Fill me, fill me, fill me!

Why can't you fill me?

This which we call "Life."

Don't let it ruin the innocence of your mind.

If it already has, no need to worry.

It may be a bee's sting of a reminder at times but that's all it'll ever be, even if that.

Once your morning walks begin, restoration is welcomed.

Witnessing that the shadows from before can no longer remain a stain.

There is One who washes all things clean. The best you will ever see!

Witnessing to testify there is a light that will never be dimmed.

THE ULTIMATE PRIZE

What's the point of words having meaning if I can't win?

What happens to everything that I have ever known?

You see, what once was out of reach is literally standing in front of me.

It seems impossible, doesn't it? No hassle. No toggle.

I was just sitting in my room when He appeared and said to me, "You will have Life."

I didn't ask questions. I simply looked forward to hearing from Him again.

I packed my bags and filled them with what was already inside, that is.

I didn't carry these bags; I simply disposed of them.

I needed more room to accept what was coming from Him.

He saved my life and became my ultimate prize.

There is nothing alive or dead, found in the today or then, that can be used as a comparison.

Show me your best. The winner will remain at rest.

WHAT HAPPENS WHEN THE SUN LEAVES

What will become of me…

When what I need to live is taken away.

In my necessity.

If what I need is not delivered, then what will become of me.

Solidarity.

I become like one of those that do fade away.

In my fragile state, as I drift through the wind, what is the next
stop that awaits me.

Immobile I become.

There is nothing to see and no one to greet.

What is this place where I am now meant to be?

The sun no longer holds its parade.

Dust will become of me.

I MUST CONFESS

I am in love.

I am tied-down, sold-out, forever-knotted to this Love.

So much so, I am willing to turn in my key.

I always thought I was dancing by myself, but I found out He was always dancing with me.

He held me tight and swung me gently across the grand floor.
He watched me as I watched the stars.

He witnessed me to glisten as I thought this view would always be pitch dark.

And I must confess, if He isn't the one I spend my eternity with as the rest, I turn in my key.

If life is not with and because of Him, I mustn't be.

If it isn't Him, the one who saved me, then a burden would be forever birthed inside of me.

Here, here is my key.

HOW FAR WILL YOU GO

This far.

What happens when you realize you've reached the end and lost the fight.

What will you do and how will you cope? Don't accept that invitation.

I know it's the worst, but don't turn the knob until you know that
indeed, it was the very end.

Someone said there is a place where we'll never die.

Wouldn't you like to walk to that place with me?

Don't fight or put up restraints. Show me how far you'll go.

YOU CAN'T BE HERE

If you don't leave, I'll go.

If you remain here, then I cannot grow.

If you stay, I won't be able to breathe.

Your stings and roots have invaded me.

I don't want to be overshadowed because of your stature over mine.

But you do not intimidate me.

I sway as you are stiffened.

I'm desired and you are plucked.

I'm sought after but you are treated to never reappear.

I'm the real thing and you are the scheme.

The Imposter, a fraud.

The author of all mischief.

But I'll tell you what, as I sway, you remain.

I'm sought after and when it comes to you, an offer is not made.

Plucked and removed you will finally get out of my way.

THE ZOO

The Whale once said to me, "Relax and swim not away."

She submerged beneath and helped me get back home safely.

A Giraffe I once climbed. I saw sights no one could ever see if they tried.

A Walrus comes out of me as I walk around chasing others with two chopsticks between my teeth.

Can I pay the price of 1 for 2?

My friend, not even the Cow could bargain at the merchants' event.

But there is one who was able to bargain for me.

He offered His finest piece.

And to you, with the perfect balanced diet of fish, nuts, insects and fruits.

Don't worry, I won't tell them your name, but I do hope to cuddle you one day.

I'VE FOUND YOU

Though you cannot see me, I can see you.

Not in a dream, and not in my reality but yours.

I come for those who yearn for me, whether they know it or not.

For every soul is on a daily conquest to find what can fill that void.

What can replace the missing piece?

Ah, but you see, this missing piece is a one and only piece.

One of a kind, never to repeat.

Cannot be made and cannot be seen.

So, now as I have found you, come and find me.

You'll never get lost for all things I do see.

I've chosen your path; you will make it safe to me.

Are you ready to see the two ends that never meet?

MY SUMMARY

To the Listener, the Reader, the Ponderer and the Receiver.

To the ones that did try, this also is for you.

And in such cases as these, to try just wasn't enough, for all you had to do was receive.

Now, where's the fight in that?

When you listen, there's a pay to attention.

There's a following and going back to practice of that which you paid your attention to.

If it was deemed good, you cash in.

But you didn't. And indeed, it was deemed good.

What's the reason behind winning the lottery and not turning in the winning ticket?

For many it remains a mystery but to one it became clear.

To "not care enough" does cost.

To not think of it as "high importance" does matter.

Life is plain and is simple.

If it is disagreed, there may be a different reality in your world, but not in mine.

LESSON #43

He did not mean for us to call it "The Let Go."

You see, He also likes to trade.

My lemon for His first-class cup of tea.

My coffee bean for His luxurious box of fine chocolates.

My empty ideas for His delicacy.

A hand-picked path for me. You cannot ever have both. There is no such thing.

All misbalance comes to an end as it cannot be forever sustained.
"Eventually" comes and visits.

Surely, without a formal announcement of arrival.

We believe that by trading that which we think to be something we could never let go of because it is all that was ever introduced, that we could not consider the better that is out there.

The infamous "I am here to tell you" says, "better" is sold rotten by trading with the world.

The "Better" that is everlasting and allows for your dreams to come true is only a trade you could never refuse.

By Him alone who created and knows you.

IT ALL MAKES SENSE

I knew I was different.

That I wanted more than what I could see.

It wasn't for me to reach yet just to dream!

What if!

So, what!

I wasn't the one with power within me.

But what if I was one of the ones? That anything they believed became a reality.

That what I envision, there wouldn't be any impossibilities.

What if that was just it?

If those around you don't comprehend what was placed inside of you, don't regard their thoughts.

The temperature may drop for some time but if you remain true and be not moved, that which you dreamed will eventually come true.

Not by my words, but by Him who placed them in you.

TIME

I am so happy!

Why?

Because He's coming for me.

You've said that for so long…

An age is just an age.

A day just a day.

Time
Life
Existence
Decisions
Durations
Expirations

A sudden stop that leads to death.

This will always come to a stop.

But where I am going next, there will not.

THE REFLECTION IN THE WATER

We're the reflection upon His eyes.

First, He sees it all.

Then, He carefully sees each one of us.

What you see, He has seen.

What He sees, we have not.

So, what is it that you do see? Describe it to me.

I see blue and I see white.

The colors of surrender sprint across my mind.

I think it could be the very sky.

Please keep this one Truth.

If you keep this one, you'll be able to reach them all.

I CAN'T HEAR YOU

There is not another way but through me!

So, I will not stop fighting for you.

Look, over here! Please, stop ignoring me.

I've come to save you, heal you, complete you!

I am here to fulfill you.

I made all things better.

Show me your wounds and let me protect you.

Don't run away, though I will not cease the chase.

Hear the words that I say.

There is a day when everything will not remain the same.

I'll keep reaching for you until the very last day.

But to all things, except for me, there is an end date.

Don't allow me to leave and you are not reaching for me.

MY NEW LIFE

If I have seen a movie, I've seen it all.

It has painted the picture for me.

That which has been portrayed, I must go after and repeat.

Nonsense.

I did not know who or what a "King" was. Not until I met Him.

I was under the spell of ignorance and lacked understanding of what a kingdom could be.

I was far from knowing anything about it.

But He tells me stories about this place.

I wasn't worthy of wearing the dresses He prepared for me, but He clothed me from His finest picks.

The best shoes, the most royal of accessories.

I thought life was as vibrant as it could be until He introduced me to it.

If you've met Him who has seen it all, then you shall truly be shown what the movies could not.

Simply, because they cannot.

I AM LOVELY BUT HE IS LOVE

He told me once, "I don't want to go, but I must leave."

I replied, "Then don't leave."

And in that very moment, as He stared into my eyes, I saw that which was unreachably deep.

He couldn't stay; He had to leave.

He's got to leave because of me.

That's when I knew.

No matter what others brought to offer, a coin or the world itself, there was not a chance in life that anything would change His mind.

Simply, that's how it had to be.

He did not choose Himself; He chose me.

There is a treat He left behind for me.

He changed me.

The one who once showed me darkness of a friend I seek.

A LAST PAGE

So, what should I say?

That the journey is worth the wait?

That is not something I must say, but you.

A child grows tall and strong.

Isn't there something to celebrate?

So, then. What should I say?

That this is impossible?

No. Nothing is impossible.

Excuse me. Let me rephrase.

Nothing is impossible to Him who can do all things.

We? We are a bit limited. So, to us, it is impossible.

Our joy is that anything we need and for anything we cannot do, there is that Someone who can simply just do.

It's what He does.

He creates, He solves, He blesses, and He does as He pleases.

He is the greatest King who ever lived!

www.ingramcontent.com/pod-product-compliance
Lightning Source LLC
LaVergne TN
LVHW010545100826
845148LV00013B/2612

9798385276431